Russell Sturgis

Results of Further Experience in the Use of the Suggestion

under Slight Hypnosis

Russell Sturgis

Results of Further Experience in the Use of the Suggestion under Slight Hypnosis

ISBN/EAN: 9783337816780

Printed in Europe, USA, Canada, Australia, Japan

Cover: Foto ©Thomas Meinert / pixelio.de

More available books at **www.hansebooks.com**

sults of Further Experience in the Use of the Suggestion under Slight Hypnosis

BY

RUSSELL STURGIS, M.D.
BOSTON, MASS.

New York Medical Record, February 25, 1899.]

BOSTON
S. J. PARKHILL & CO., PRINTERS
226 FRANKLIN STREET
1899

RESULTS OF FURTHER EXPERIENCE IN THE USE OF THE SUGGESTION UNDER SLIGHT HYPNOSIS.

BY RUSSELL STURGIS, M.D., BOSTON.

In a paper written not long ago [1] I endeavored to frame a theory by which I thought we might arrive at a clearer understanding of the use of the suggestion given during the lighter degrees of hypnosis. I gave my reasons for supposing that there was a common ground of implantation of a fixed idea and of an idea given during hypnosis, namely, that part of the mind to which is relegated the inception of the performance of habitual actions of the body, and of habitual or involuntary processes of mind. I reported cases illustrative of the possible manner of implantation of fixed ideas and of the method of giving suggestion in such cases.

Since writing my paper I have tried to find, if possible, some symptom common to those cases in which it has seemed to me advisable to use suggestion under hypnosis. I hoped that by finding such symptom, or group of symptoms, there might appear some scheme or plan according to which the suggestion might be given, thus placing the use of the suggestion on a more scientific basis than has hitherto been done, so far as I am aware. I think that every one who has had much to do with cases of psychasthenia has felt that there are certain symptoms that are almost pathognomonic of this condition. By such symptoms he recognizes his cases as being psychasthenic. It will be my endeavor to show that these common symptoms may be traced

[1] New York Medical Record, February 17, 1894.

to a certain definite symptom which may be called the main. I am well aware that I may be utterly mistaken in my views regarding this main symptom, but I strongly feel that every attempt toward a concrete rather than a general conception of psychasthenic conditions is a step in advance, and, should my theory seem untenable, I shall be only too glad to change my present views or to shape them to any other theory which may tend to put the treatment of mental conditions by mental therapeutics on a firmer scientific basis than at present seems to exist.

My aim, then, in the present paper, is to show that there is a possibility of the existence of an early mental symptom or morbid idea common to all conditions of brain fag or psychasthenia; also to show that the continuance of the mental state which gave rise to this symptom or idea may give rise to those symptoms which lead us to make our diagnosis of psychasthenia. I shall try further to show that this main symptom or idea may be combated by a definite main suggestion, and that as the secondary symptoms or ideas may be traced to amplification of the main idea, so secondary suggestions logically connected with the main suggestion may be used to combat the secondary ideas. I shall give a couple of sets of suggestions illustrative of this method of eliminating the morbid ideas. A report of a small number of cases, and of deductions which may be made from them, will close the paper.

Since the summer of 1894 it has seemed to me that one of the first, if not the very first, symptom of psychasthenia is the lack of power to control the train of thought properly or normally. Now the power to control a train of thought seems to me dependent on some other power. As a train of thought must, presumably, be composed of a combination or sequence of certain separate ideas, there must be some power of assorting those ideas which are proper to enter into the composition of a normal train of thought ; of accepting the suitable and of rejecting those ideas that are unsuitable to such normal or healthy train. This power of choice must, in turn, be dependent on some other quality of mind by which is appreciated the ratio of value between two presented ideas, in terms of their acceptance or rejection as component parts of a normal train of thought. It seems to me that this power of appreciating without conscious mental effort the correct ratio of value between ideas presented to the mind is probably the outcome of deductions which have been drawn from results of former personal experiences. For instance : the idea of the probability of a chair being able to walk off on its four legs is one which to the normal mind is so preposterous, so at variance with the results of past experience, that, without conscious effort of the intellect, we at once make choice of the idea that such a performance on the part of the chair is absurd, and at once exclude the idea that such movements are possible. Yet such an idea regarding locomotion might be received not only as possible, but even as probable, by a mind unbalanced ; there might be not only difficulty in choosing between the ideas as presented, but the power of appreciating the ratio of value between the two ideas might be so impaired, that the probability of voluntary motion of the chair might seem the idea most consistent with the truth, and might therefore be accepted as the idea most worthy of, consideration. For this power by which we unconsciously appreciate the ratio of value and as unconsciously make our choice, there seems to be no descriptive term. "Common-sense" describes it fairly, but is rather colloquial for use. "Will" is hardly the word to use, as most people confuse the idea of "will" with "volition" (" *Vouloir, c'est choisir pour agir*" [1]); yet, inasmuch as the word "will," taken as meaning *unconscious* choice made preliminary to action, is linked very closely with the power of appreciating ideas at their proper value, I have made use of the word "will" to denote that power as well, and have always described it as distinct from "volition," which may be taken as representing the *conscious* choice made previous to action. This word "will," then, I have taken simply as a matter of convenience, as representing not only that quality which makes it possible for the normal mind to ignore at once any idea which in the light of ordinary experience would seem to be absurd, but also to represent the function so closely allied to, and preceding that of unconsciously choosing : the ability to appreciate the ordinary ratio of value between two ideas.

How are we to recognize weakening of the unconscious will? There are two groups of symptoms denoting such weakening. The first consists of symptoms which the patient cannot explain to himself, the origin of which is absolutely beyond his power to appreciate unless it be explained to him. The second consists of symptoms which he can himself recognize as having direct bearing on his condition.

The first group is composed of symptoms of two classes : those represented by mental apathy and those represented by mental erethism. Though so diverse, these symptoms may both be shown to result from weakness of the unconscious will. Bearing in mind that such weakness means loss of ap-

[1] Ribot: Maladies de la Volonté.

preciation of the ratio of value between two presented ideas, and also subsequent embarrassment of choice, the matter becomes clear. In the condition of apathy, ideas of action are, relatively to ideas of inaction, of much less value than under normal conditions. Ideas of inactivity therefore predominate, and a condition in which the mind no longer responds to the stimulus of the ordinary interests of daily life results. Not only are the stimuli to action of less effect than ordinary, but the affections are frequently blunted during this apathetic period. This blunting of the affections seems to be due to the fact that in all probability, the affections being dependent on mental activity and alertness, a diminution in activity results in diminution of the affections. The condition of mental erethism, in like manner, is due to weakening of ideas of inaction, that is, of inhibitory ideas, due, in turn, to the error in the sense of proportion between ideas of action and of inaction. Ideas of action are taken as of greater importance than their contrary, and therefore any idea may become a spur to mental activity, such mental activity being along lines of no practical value. Patients are emotional, and in every respect the reverse of those in the apathetic condition. For neither of these conditions of apathy or of erethism can the patient account. In one case he knows only that he cannot interest himself in things as he did. He feels his mind " dead within him," as I have heard it expressed, and cannot tell why he should feel so, or what has changed him from a person naturally bright and interested, into this dull, apathetic creature. No more can he account for the constant spur to energy, for this gadfly that drives him from one thing to another without opportunity for rest. He simply notices that he is incapable of quiet of mind, that his thoughts are constantly active in one direction or another, and that nothing but vexation may be the result of this forced mental activity.

Now it seems to me that consequent on weakening of will, there must come weakening of the power of spontaneous or passive attention, which, in turn, must be followed by diminished power of the voluntary attention. I suppose that, as a rule, this weakening of the voluntary attention is the first mental symptom of which the patient is conscious, and represents the second group of symptoms spoken of above. He cannot explain to himself the cause of his apathetic condition, for instance, for he cannot realize the condition of aboulia, or weakness of the unconscious will, upon which this depends. But when he finds that he cannot concentrate his mind for more than a very brief period at a time, he appreciates the condition as one dependent upon weakened power of the voluntary attention. This weakening of the voluntary attention he notices also in his effort to exclude voluntarily from his mind, ideas which obtrude ; ideas which his reason tells him are preposterous. He recognizes that they are preposterous, unnatural, foolish, or what not ; but inasmuch as they have been admitted by the unconscious will as ideas which are worthy of attention ; inasmuch as they have not been rejected as absurd — as they should have been — without mental effort on the part of the patient : when they are perceived by the mind, they have the guise of, or are analogous to, trains of thought, the result of many experiences — in short, as due to habit. As habits of thought are beyond the control of the reasoning powers, so these are not controlled by the reason, and cannot be excluded by volition, or by any conscious mental effort. The outgrowth of any persistent idea which is recognized by the reason as absurd, may become exuberant; and such exuberance is limited only by the patient's imagination. The most fantastic ideas regarding the significance of bodily sensations and symptoms are frequently met. We also often see patients worrying over the trivial affairs of daily life, which their judgment tells them are absurd. Yet, inasmuch as the sense of proportion has been lost, or weakened, the trivial things have not been excluded, as they should have been, without any conscious mental effort ; they are given such prominence as they would normally have were they worthy of consideration and were they so classed by the unconscious mind. The obvious idea that presents itself to a patient with weakened voluntary attention, is one of some damage done to his mind ; and consequently, loss of confidence in himself and in his brain power, is to him the logical outcome of this weakened condition of the voluntary attention. By self-analysis this feeling of incompetency may be increased, so that the patient may self-limit his mental powers in whatever direction and to whatever degree may seem to him logical and natural. Not only may he fancy his mental powers to be very much limited. but he may further elaborate the idea of mental failure and may infer that he necessarily must be on the road to insanity.

I suppose it is more than probable that at some period, more or less remotely following that at which the brain became fagged, (with consequent failure of will power). there comes into existence what one may call a habit psychosis. By this one means that the symptoms directly due to the original brain fag or psychasthenia may still remain. as the results of habits of thought. We then have a condition of pseudo-psychasthenia. The will has recovered its tone, but, as that loss of tone was not recognized by the patient, as such, at the time of the fag, for the same reason its return to the normal is not appreciated, and therefore, until this condition of pseudo-psychasthenia is explained to him, he can make no use of the increased or normal will power. The analogy between symptoms of physical fatigue and those of mental may be used to explain to a patient this condition of pseudo-psychasthenia.

Suppose that a man who has never known bodily fatigue, and who can walk ten miles without feeling any other effect than the pleasurable sense of exercise performed, walks fifty. That night he goes to bed footsore and stiff. Next morning he wakes, attempts, as usual, to spring out of bed and finds that there is no spring in him. His legs are stiff and lame, he gets his feet to the floor, finds them sore, gets back into bed and says to himself, "I have ruined my legs by that walk, they are no longer supple and strong. I can't bear my weight on my feet without pain. That walk has put an end to my walking for the future." He keeps his bed for ten days or so. A friend comes in, hears his story, makes fun of him for thinking that he has damaged himself in any way, says, "You were tired, that is all, there is not anything the matter with you ; you can walk all right if you think you can." The man thinks otherwise, but, as he is tired of his bed, after his friend has gone he thinks he might as well try to walk. He tries. and fails. His legs, now weak from disuse, refuse to support him. He crawls back to bed with the *experience* now, that he is damaged for life. Now ensues a period of further inactivity, the legs meanwhile growing smaller and smaller, weaker and weaker. There comes to him another friend. The old story, now backed up by experience, is told. Says the friend, "Yet your experience, as you call it, is all wrong. Your legs were never damaged. Your second failure was due not to damage but to disuse. Your legs are healthy, the muscles are all there, simply waiting to be used. Come, try a step or two with me. I will come again in the afternoon and we will try some more. After a little while you will find that you can walk as well as ever." All goes well, strength returns and the man is happy. More than that; his *real* experience of fatigue has taken away, probably, any chance that in future, should he again suffer the first symptoms of bodily over-exertion, he will think that there is permanent damage as a necessary result. Step by step we may follow the analogy : the first symptoms of mental fatigue, the expansion of ideas of incompetency, the appeal without explanation, and, finally, the thing explained. How many persons are there who know just what are the effects of mental fatigue? Until these effects are recognized as such, is it any wonder that temporary insufficiency is mistaken for permanent damage?

This condition of pseudo-psychasthenia then, is directly due to that weakness of will which followed the original mental strain or shock. This weakening of the will should have been temporary, but the *symptoms* of such weakening having been kept in prominence by the very faulty habit of thought which itself was a symptom of weakness of will, there still exists an apparent, though not true, weakness of will — a weakness due to disuse and distrust. By reason of this weakness from disuse, it is possible still to have symptoms originally due to weakness from fatigue; namely, lines of thought which are insistent, though absurd; physical sensations modified more or less, according to whether greater or less stress is laid on this or that symptom ; experience due to memories or associations, in the same way, more or less perverted.

I give three examples of causes of morbid blushing to illustrate my point that a symptom may originate and may be kept in existence by perverted experience, due to inability to control the line of thought, which inability is, in its turn, due to weakness of the unconscious will.

In one case a supposed cause for shame occurring many years before gives rise to expectation of blushing and to consequent blushing. In another case an idea that there exists a peculiarity due to heredity — such peculiarity being afterward explained to himself as faulty vasomotor innervation — gives rise to expectation and blushing. In a third case fancied failure, and the idea that others might think him of small account, result in embarrassment and blushing.

In the first instance there was really no cause for shame, and the act that caused the fancied shame dates back twenty-six years. In the second, the idea that he was not like other boys, in that his experience did not teach him that he would outgrow the habit of blushing, is the idea upon which undue stress is laid. In the third, the idea that a failure due to physical causes, might be interpreted as due to mental deficiency or stupidity, is the erroneous conclusion.

In cases of pseudo-psychasthenia it is frequently noticed that there may be no weakening of the voluntary attention at all. The mind may be kept on the subject in hand, reading is easy, and so on. The mental or even physical symptoms are due to weakness of the unconscious will from disuse along certain lines only. In these cases we generally get the history of loss of power of concentration at some time closely following the original strain. Now this pseudo-psychasthenic condition, which is recognized by the symptoms of psychasthenia persisting long after the will should have recovered its normal strength, affords just the class of cases in which suggestion seems of value.

Assuming, then, that there is in the case of every normal person a will by which not only does he appreciate the proper or ordinary ratio of value between ideas, but also by which he makes choice of one of those ideas as proper under given conditions, and, in addition, assuming that this appreciation and choice are both processes of mind unperceived by the personality at the time of their activity, in what way can we strengthen this will when, on account of strain or through disuse, it may have become weakened? As this will is one of the unperceived and therefore automatic powers of the mind, and if, as I have before tried to show, there is probability that the suggestion under hypnosis reaches the same part of the mind in which automatic processes arise, then a suggestion that the will *is* strong should strengthen the will. As a matter of fact, such a suggestion seems to do this very thing. If a patient presents himself suffering from the effects of aboulia, such as loss of power of initiative, aprosexia, loss of confidence in himself and in his abilities, and possibly with further development of any of these ideas of incompetence, what is the course to pursue if you mean to use suggestion? After letting the patient detail his woes I generally endeavor to explain to him the conditions subsequent to brain fag. Now if I am pretty sure that the strain was undergone so long ago that there has been plenty of time for recovery of the brain from the fatigue, in other words, if I think I have to deal with a pseudo-psychasthenic

case, I explain that while the condition (the worrying train of thought and its consequences) was due
originally to weakness of the will, yet now the will
has probably recovered its tone, but may be handicapped in usefulness because the patient believes it
still weakened by the original strain; so that the
symptoms, due originally to a weakness of will, are
now due to habit alone ; and that suggestion, by removing the habit of thought, will leave the will un-
hampered to do its work properly. This method has
been criticised on the ground that I am giving a patient a new fixed idea. Quite right ; if it be a new
fixed idea, it seems to me a good one, and he cannot
come to much harm who has, solidly fixed in his
mind, the idea that his will is strong enough at any
time to control his train of thought.

The main suggestion which I have used since
October 28, 1894, is as follows : " Your (unconscious)
will is strong enough, at any time, to control your
thoughts and to keep them in natural channels."
The term " natural channels," by mutual understanding between myself and my patients, is taken to
mean the train of thought which the normal person
deems natural under given conditions. I will now
give a couple of illustrative cases. It will be noticed
that each patient was handicapped, so far as his
work was concerned ; one by self-limitation as to the
amount of work that could be done, the other by
the fear lest a previous condition of ill health might
supervene unless there should be better sleep. In
both cases mental strain due to overwork and worry
was responsible for the beginning of the train of
symptoms which they presented on consulting me ;
but in both cases the overstrain had taken place
some years previously, and presumably the line of
thought existing at the time of consulting me was

due rather to a habit than to an existing condition of brain fag. The use of a main suggestion to combat the main idea or symptom, and the use of secondary suggestions by which the secondary symptoms were fought, I will try to show.

CASE I. Lawyer, married, forty-four years. Present trouble dates from 1881. A gradual psychasthenic condition came on as the result of considerable worry and overwork. This condition was characterized by diminished power of concentration, and evolution, later, of the idea that he had damaged his brain power by overwork and by certain excesses. In 1884 he got a fright about the condition of his heart, his physician leading him to infer that he had mitral disease, a condition later proved not to exist. He became so wretched that in 1884 he went South and engaged in out-of-door work, continuing this till 1893, when he came North again. Instead of finding himself able to go to work again at the law after this long rest, he found that he could work no longer nor better than before he went away. He was naturally much discouraged when he found that he could work no more than three hours a day. If he worked more than that time his powers of concentration seemed to desert him entirely, and not only that, but his night was wretched, disturbed by terrifying dreams; and next morning a strange tension in the head which troubled him after work, persisted in spite of the night spent in bed. After having stood this sort of thing for more than a year, he consulted me on December 24, 1895. There was nothing particularly noticeable in his appearance, nor was his family history of much importance. He was in pretty fair bodily condition, and consulted me simply because he wanted the power to work as well as other men.

By that he meant power to work in his office from nine in the morning till five in the afternoon, with an hour out for lunch. He wanted to feel that he could enjoy himself in the evening, free from the idea that he would have a horrible night should he increase his hours of work. He wanted no more pain in his head from the amount of work above mentioned than any normal man would suffer — meaning by that, none. It was pointed out to him that he had probably made the mistake of assuming that the difficulty in concentrating, due to disuse of his intellect while he was working in the lumber camp down South, was not due to mental degeneration ; that the mind had become but a bit stiff in its working, from disuse; and that he had made a limit for himself as to his power for work, by drawing deductions from the false premise that the brain had deteriorated in consequence of the severe strain of nine years ago. On close questioning it was found that there was also the idea present that some deterioration had followed certain excesses just prior to his breakdown in 1881. This seems to be a clear case of loss of confidence due to temporary loss of the power of concentration. This loss of confidence was followed in turn by the fixed idea that the brain had been damaged, with corresponding physical symptoms, such as he would expect from such damage, namely, painful sensations in the head and poor sleep. All this was explained to him. In this case recovery was complete and rapid, the report, one month after treatment, being that he could work from nine till five as proposed, and that since the first fortnight after beginning to work, there had been no tension in the head, and there had been good sleep. The improvement was lasting.

The suggestions were in this case the *main*, " Your will is strong enough at any time to control your thoughts, and to keep them in natural channels ; *second*, " Therefore you know that no excesses nor overtaxing of your intellect in the past has diminished your natural power for mental or physical work. You can sleep, therefore, at night like any healthy person, and a reasonable amount of brain work cannot disturb your rest at night." It will be noticed that in the suggestions, no mention was made of the painful tension in the head. This was understood as included in the phrase " diminished your power for mental and physical work." The painful tension in the head was probably due to an idea of what sort of sensation in one's head would naturally result from brain overwork — in other words, he had evolved this symptom for himself, supposing that excessive brain work would have as result pain or tension in the brain ; just as excessive muscular work would give rise to soreness and stiffness of the muscles. It seemed best to make a special suggestion regarding sleep, for we wanted to include in that the idea of recuperation from the fatigue of the previous day, by means of that refreshing sleep, free from terrifying dreams, · which is natural to the healthy person. In this case, the suggestions were given, under light hypnosis, five separate times : 15 minutes, 30 minutes, 30 minutes, 45 minutes and 45 minutes.

CASE II. Teacher, single, thirty-six years. Father and mother both strong and well. Always stood well in her classes at school, and meant to be a teacher. In 1882 was obliged to leave the Normal School before getting her diploma, facial neuralgia and a general break-down being the cause. No insomnia at that time. In 1883 she taught school, but broke down again after six weeks. This time insomnia first appeared. For eight or nine years she had to be at home, idle, incapable of teaching, or even of any sustained thought, and lacking the power of initiative. Toward the end of 1891 she began to help her mother in the housework. In 1892 she began some gymnasium work at home, but had to give it up in three weeks on account of the return of insomnia. At that time she could read and study but little, on account of difficulty of application. Early in 1893 she took up work in the Posse Gymnasium and felt much better for it, being able to study and to sleep well. Between 1893 and 1895 she had classes in gymnastics at home and in a neighboring town, keeping well and sleeping well. In 1895 she took charge of gymnasium work, as instructress, in A. She did well there, being little troubled by insomnia, working hard, but taking a good rest in the summer. In the autumn of 1897 she went to the Normal School in B., as superintendent of the gymnasium. She was a stranger there, and felt her loneliness much. Her work from 1893 to 1897 had been accompanied by physical exertion, and she had felt well. At B., on the contrary, she had little exercise, but superintended the work of others with the view of making them instructors.

Present condition. — Appears well nourished, and in fair physical shape. She gets to sleep fairly well, but wakes early, and can't get to sleep again. Has tried various means of getting sleep, including the ordinary hypnotics. On close questioning, there appears to be little cause for any particular worry, other than that for the consequences of the insomnia. She is subject to sudden fits of depression, which are accompanied by epigastric discomfort, but digestion seems to be well performed. After a nap this depression and discomfort will frequently disappear. She regards fear of insomnia as the only drawback to her success. She is sure that if she could only sleep she would be all right. She has a certain amount of loss of confidence and some aprosexia; is much discouraged at the prospect of having to give up her work, and fears that she may relapse into the condition in which she was in 1881–1892. Here we have a case of very decided fear lest there should be a return of a condition from which she has been free for about five years. The experience of the last five years goes for nothing. There are symptoms of a psychasthenic condition, as shown by loss of confidence, aprosexia and lack of initiative. This last symptom became of considerable importance immediately after the treatment, and I think that probably had that phase of the mental condition been treated at the time the suggestions were given, the recovery would have been quicker. I was inclined to think that the unusual sense of loneliness, which she mentioned as being an element of discomfort at B., was due to lack of confidence, and therefore I gave her a special suggestion for regaining that confidence. As in her case the insomnia seemed to her to be the most important symptom, the suggestion for its relief was given as being directly consequent upon the main suggestion. The following were the suggestions: *Main suggestion*, the same as in Case I; *secondary*, "Therefore no worries that you may have had can keep you awake at night; so you can sleep at night like any healthy woman. Therefore you have confidence in your abilities." The suggestions were given nine times. The patient seemed very reluctant to go back to B., though I repeatedly urged that she should. She would make up her mind to go, and then the fear lest she might have to give up her work again would deter her from making the move. For a month she hung about, now sleeping well, and then again poorly, until she was finally persuaded that no opportunity to find whether the suggestions had done any good would be obtained, until she should put herself in the position to do some work. On the urgent solicitation of the principal of the school at B., backed by me, she returned, just one month after the last time that the suggestions had been given her. It has seemed to me that this delay was due to an aboulia, and that perhaps a mistake was made in not laying more stress on that particular phase. All came right shortly after her arrival. On December 5th she wrote : "I taught Thursday and Friday (my return was on Monday), and slept better than for a long time." On January 3d : "I am still at B., you see. Conditions have been very favorable to me " (by which she means that she has fallen in with some very pleasant people, that her work was appreciated, etc.), "and I hope I am well started in my work." May 1st : "I am very well indeed now, and flourishing on hard but very enjoyable work." January 2. 1899 : "I am very well indeed, better than at any time since my first prostration." Sundays were irksome to her for some time, because there was no work to be done, and she seemed to sleep less well on Sunday night than on the nights that succeeded work. This same peculiarity I have noted in a somewhat similar case.

TABLE OF CASES.

	Whole number.	Successes.	Failures.	Per cent of successes.
Class A	31	20	11	64.5%
Class B	20	11	9	55 0%
Classes A and B	51	31	20	60.78%

Class A includes all cases in which the mental symptoms were especially prominent, that is, cases in which I have been consulted because of the presence of painful or insistent ideas. There were, of course, in most of these cases physical symptoms, but the patients came because they were wretched in mind, and regarded their physical symptoms as of secondary importance.

Class B includes those cases that consulted me because of physical symptoms, some of which they called " nervous." In these cases, although it was not usually difficult to detect the mental cause of the physical symptoms, yet the mental state did not obtrude itself on the patient's attention, and, in fact, he may have scouted the idea that his physical symptoms were in any way dependent on the mental condition.

In classing the cases as successes or failures, I have tried to be conservative regarding successes. They are regarded as such only when relief from a painful train of thought or other symptom has been so quickly obtained, and so long continued, that relief seems, without doubt, to have been the result of suggestion under hypnosis.

As failures, are classed all doubtful successes — those in which relief was so long coming that it was uncertain whether relief was not due to suggestion in the waking state or to other means of cure addressed to the general condition. Among failures are also included cases of relapse and of short-lived improvement.

That I have no larger number of cases to report during the four years following February, 1894, is partly explained by the fact that I have used hypnosis in as few cases as possible, because I do not like to employ it, feeling, as I do, that implanting an idea in the mind of a person who is artificially rendered unusually susceptible to suggestion, carries with it a grave responsibility which I do not care to shoulder oftener than I can help. Another reason for the small number is, that working in the field in which mental processes are concerned, one acquires a certain readiness of judgment and facility of expression that enables him to use to advantage suggestion in the waking state. Dr. Morton Prince,[3] in a recent paper, has called attention to this method which he calls the " educational treatment," its aim, of course, being to explain to your patient his condition so that he can understand it, in that way removing his fears regarding what, to him, is an inexplicable complex of mental symptoms, thus giving to him hope, the best of all tonics. This treatment, together with attention to the general health, has proved for several years so satisfactory, that I prefer using it alone if there be time. I never use hypnosis in addition unless time should be very limited, on account of the patient coming from a distance, or for some other reason that may force me to its use ; as in the case of a patient who insists that he has come for that particular treatment alone, and who wants it used, unless I am to assure him that its use is unsuitable in his case. In none of the cases has there been dependence upon the suggestion under hypnosis alone. In all the educational treatment has been used to a greater or less degree ; the suggestion under slight hypnosis has been used as a time-saver, or for some other sufficient reason.

It may be asked why, if the hypothesis that psychasthenic symptoms are due to impairment of will, the percentage of success is not greater. In the first place, from my inexperience, I have prob-

[3] Proceedings Massachusetts Medical Society, June, 1898.

ably used suggestion under slight hypnosis in unsuitable cases. *Second*, The patients may not have
been in the receptive condition at all. This is possible, as being unwilling to induce hypnosis to the
deeper degrees, which induce the features charac-
teristic of those degrees, I have as my only guide
the apparent willingness of a person to lie perfectly
quiet, with closed eyes, for an hour or so. This
willingness may be due to complaisance on the part
of the patient, and he may not really have been
" under control." *Third*, I have put all my doubtful successes into the list of failures. A comparison
of the classes A and B shows that the use of suggestion in the first class is somewhat more satisfactory
than in the second. This was what I suspected
before I analyzed my cases. I am inclined to think
that those cases only are amenable to suggestion in
which you may reasonably hope that many iterations
of your own beliefs as to the patient's condition
might, after a considerable interval of time, bring
him to agree with your view of the case. In other
words, if you can't conceive the probability of being
able to talk him out of his beliefs, I am inclined to
think that you cannot get the beliefs out of his
head by any kind of suggestion. Considerable press-
ure was brought to bear in a case of paranoia of
long standing, and I was induced, though unwilling,
to use suggestion. I made a complete failure. I
don't believe that that person could have been
talked out of her peculiar belief had she been talked
to, and reasoned with, for years. The so-called
cases of pain habit have also been very stubborn,
and, though in one case there was relief to a certain
extent, yet it must be classed among the unsuccessful.
Regarding the effects of suggestion under slight
hypnosis, I have noticed, to a slight degree, what

Pierre Janet [4] calls the "need of guidance." After
patients have been helped they sometimes seem to
have an inordinate respect for one's judgment, and
will ask advice on all sorts of unimportant matters.
Whether this is due to the condition of hypnosis in
which they have been, or whether it is due to grati-
tude or not, I do not know. When, in my judgment, they ought to depend on themselves, I plainly
tell them that I shall not help them any longer in
the direction in which I think they are able to help
themselves, insisting that they are well enough to go
alone; tell them that they must not come to see me
for a fortnight or so. Being thus thrown on their
own resources, they find that they can do for themselves what was easier for them to have done by
some one else, and they gain confidence every day.
The wrench is very much like that which a patient
gets when, after a long illness, a nurse is dismissed.
The patient finds it very difficult, at first, to do for
himself and to think for himself. In some cases
the reverse is true : self-confidence returns early,
and the patient seems to think that he has got
well, quite by himself, and that the suggestions
seem to be only a bit of advice given him in a friendly
way. I rather think that these diverse conditions are
a matter of temperament. The "taking" of the
main suggestion is never noticed, as such, I think.
We are none of us conscious of this power of appreciating the ratio of which I have spoken above.
The power is there, but its use passes unnoticed ;
so it would be strange if in cases in which the
power has been weakened, return of normal strength
should be noted. As we are dealing with trains of
thought which are, so to speak, automatic, a patient
on the way to recovery never says to himself, "Such

[4] Janet : Névroses et Idées fixes.

and such a suggestion has become a belief to me."
He says, rather, "Why, it seems to me that it is
some time since that old idea has troubled me," or
something of that sort. He may not notice that he
has confidence in himself to any greater degree
than before treatment, but the way in which he looks
at life and forms his judgments shows his physician
and his own friends that he is more and more like
himself. Little phrases in his letters will tell the
story of a changed current of thought and consequent approach to the normal.

Regarding improvement after psychasthenia, my
impression borne out by observation, is, that with
full explanation of the condition to the patient, and
subsequent suggestion along the line of abnormal
thought, a person, in many cases, may be stronger
in mind, and better able to stand another strain, than
before his psychasthenia. This seems to me reasonable, because if again subjected to strain, the first
symptom noticed, generally a weakening of the
attention, can no longer frighten him as it did.
Realizing the symptom at its true value, he takes
it as a temporary sign of strain, and is not likely to
build a fanciful structure involving insanity and
failure of mind, upon what he has been taught to
regard as a weak foundation. In this respect I
think that the educational treatment is of the very
greatest importance.

Conclusions. — It seems to me that there is an
early mental symptom in psychasthenia, unnoticed
by the patient — the main symptom. This is an
inability to appreciate the ordinarily accepted ratio
of value between ideas presented to the mind. Consequent to this inability comes aboulia and the other
well-recognized symptoms of mental strain. This
inability to appreciate, can be restored by a main

suggestion ; and secondary suggestions, logically
dependent upon the main, may be used to combat
the secondary symptoms or ideas. The use of the
suggestion, by which I mean ideas impressed upon
a person's mind according to some definite plan, as
regards the mental symptoms, and not any haphazard
talking to, or any friendly talk with, the patient, is
of great value in the treatment of psychasthenia.
In fact, such cases are those that can probably be
most helped by suggestion. Cases of paranoia,
cases of any of the different forms of insanity, seem
to me to be unsuitable for its use.

44 THE FENWAY, February, 1899.